BY THOMAS K. ADAMSON

THE MIAMI
DOLPHINS
STORY

BELLWETHER MEDIA · MINNEAPOLIS, MN

™

Are you ready to take it to the extreme? Torque books thrust you into the action-packed world of sports, vehicles, mystery, and adventure. These books may include dirt, smoke, fire, and chilling tales. **WARNING**: read at your own risk.

This edition first published in 2017 by Bellwether Media, Inc.

No part of this publication may be reproduced in whole or in part without written permission of the publisher. For information regarding permission, write to Bellwether Media, Inc., Attention: Permissions Department, 5357 Penn Avenue South, Minneapolis, MN 55419.

Library of Congress Cataloging-in-Publication Data

Names: Adamson, Thomas K., 1970- author.
Title: The Miami Dolphins Story / by Thomas K. Adamson.
Description: Minneapolis, MN : Bellwether Media, Inc., 2017. | Series:
   Torque: NFL Teams | Includes bibliographical references and index.
Identifiers: LCCN 2015047968 | ISBN 9781626173712 (hardcover : alk. paper)
Subjects: LCSH: Miami Dolphins (Football team)–History–Juvenile literature.
Classification: LCC GV956.M47 A43 2017 | DDC 796.332/640975938–dc23
LC record available at http://lccn.loc.gov/2015047968

Printed in the United States of America, North Mankato, MN.

TABLE OF CONTENTS

On December 28, 2008, the Miami Dolphins face their biggest **rival**. They are in New York to play the Jets. With a victory, they will win the **division** title.

FORMER RIVAL

The Jets cut Chad Pennington after the 2007 season. He was determined to beat the Jets as a Dolphin.

André Goodman

In the third quarter, the Dolphins are behind by 3 points. **Quarterback** Chad Pennington leads his **offense** down the field.

Anthony Fasano

Pennington throws a 20-yard pass to the end zone. **Tight end** Anthony Fasano turns and makes the catch while falling down. He hangs on to the ball. Touchdown!

The final score is 24 to 17. The Dolphins make the **playoffs**!

SCORING TERMS

END ZONE
the area at each end of a football field; a team scores by entering the opponent's end zone with the football.

EXTRA POINT
a score that occurs when a kicker kicks the ball between the opponent's goal posts after a touchdown is scored; 1 point.

FIELD GOAL
a score that occurs when a kicker kicks the ball between the opponent's goal posts; 3 points.

SAFETY
a score that occurs when a player on offense is tackled behind his own goal line; 2 points for defense.

TOUCHDOWN
a score that occurs when a team crosses into its opponent's end zone with the football; 6 points.

TWO-POINT CONVERSION
a score that occurs when a team crosses into its opponent's end zone with the football after scoring a touchdown; 2 points.

The Dolphins' best seasons have had **legendary** quarterbacks. Bob Griese led the Dolphins to two **Super Bowl** wins.

Dan Marino

Dan Marino became one of the greatest National Football League (NFL) quarterbacks in history. He was the first player to reach 60,000 passing yards!

The Dolphins play home games in Miami
Gardens, Florida. Their home stadium opened
in 1987.

Stadium improvements were made from
2014 to 2016. It now has new seats and video
boards. A new **canopy** shades most fans
while the grass field still gets sun.

MIAMI GARDENS, FLORIDA

N
W + E
S

Stadium under former name

The Dolphins play in the American Football **Conference** (AFC) East Division. Their main rivals are the Buffalo Bills and the New York Jets.

Many games against the Jets are hard-fought. In January 1983, the teams met in the playoffs. The Dolphins beat the Jets to go to Super Bowl 17.

NFL DIVISIONS

AFC

AFC NORTH

BALTIMORE **RAVENS**

CINCINNATI **BENGALS**

CLEVELAND **BROWNS**

PITTSBURGH **STEELERS**

AFC EAST

BUFFALO **BILLS**

MIAMI **DOLPHINS**

NEW ENGLAND **PATRIOTS**

NEW YORK **JETS**

AFC SOUTH

HOUSTON **TEXANS**

INDIANAPOLIS **COLTS**

JACKSONVILLE **JAGUARS**

TENNESSEE **TITANS**

AFC WEST

DENVER **BRONCOS**

KANSAS CITY **CHIEFS**

OAKLAND **RAIDERS**

SAN DIEGO **CHARGERS**

NFC

NFC NORTH

CHICAGO
BEARS

DETROIT
LIONS

GREEN BAY
PACKERS

MINNESOTA
VIKINGS

NFC EAST

DALLAS
COWBOYS

GIANTS

PHILADELPHIA
EAGLES

WASHINGTON
REDSKINS

NFC SOUTH

FALCONS

CAROLINA
PANTHERS

NEW ORLEANS
SAINTS

BUCCANEERS

NFC WEST

CARDINALS

LOS ANGELES
RAMS

SAN FRANCISCO
49ERS

SEATTLE
SEAHAWKS

In 1966, the Dolphins became the first **expansion team** of the American Football League (AFL). They joined the NFL in 1970. That year, the Dolphins hired Don Shula as head coach. In his first season, the team earned a **winning record** and went to the playoffs!

1966 season

Don Shula

PERFECT SEASON

The Dolphins made history in 1972. They had a perfect season and won Super Bowl 7!

Under Shula, the team went to three Super Bowls in a row. Of those, they won Super Bowls 7 and 8. Shula also coached the team to Super Bowls 17 and 19 in the 1980s.

WINNING COACH

Don Shula set the record for most-ever wins as an NFL coach. A total of 274 of those 347 wins were with the Dolphins!

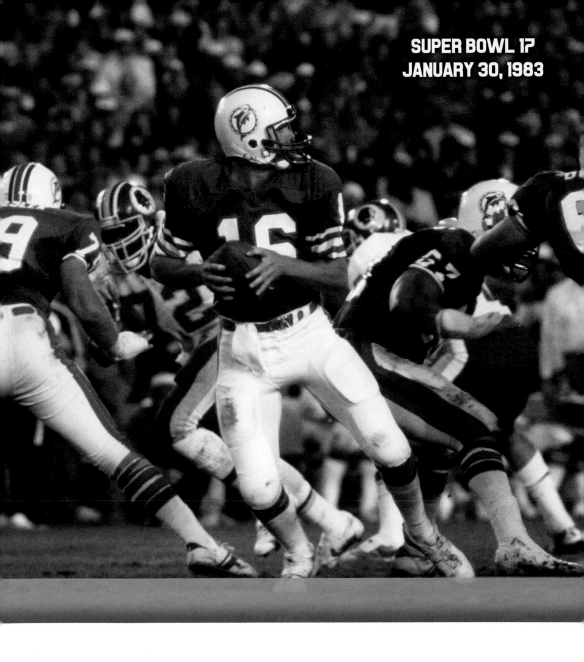

The Dolphins have had rough seasons, too. In 2007, they won only one game. But the next year, they had an 11-5 season and made the playoffs!

DOLPHINS
TIMELINE

1973

Won Super Bowl 7, beating the Washington Redskins after completing a perfect 1972 season

14   FINAL SCORE   **7**

1965

Approved as an expansion team by the AFL

1970

Named Don Shula as head coach

1972

Played in Super Bowl 6, but lost to the Dallas Cowboys

3   FINAL SCORE   **24**

1971

Won first playoff game in double overtime, beating the Kansas City Chiefs (27-24); set record for the longest NFL game in history (82 minutes and 40 seconds).

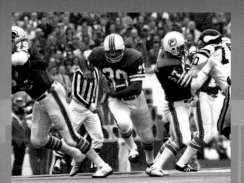

1974

Won Super Bowl 8, beating the Minnesota Vikings

24   FINAL SCORE   **7**

1984

Played in Super Bowl 19, but lost to the San Francisco 49ers

16   FINAL SCORE   **38**

1982

Played in Super Bowl 17, but lost to the Washington Redskins

17   FINAL SCORE   **27**

2000

Celebrated the retirement of Hall-of-Fame quarterback Dan Marino

DOLPHINS

Two Hall-of-Fame quarterbacks spent their entire careers with the Dolphins. In the 1970s, Bob Griese brought the team to its first three Super Bowls.

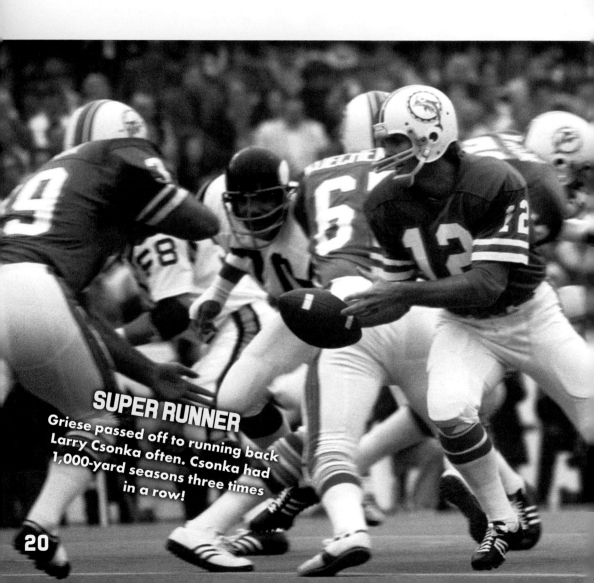

SUPER RUNNER
Griese passed off to running back Larry Csonka often. Csonka had 1,000-yard seasons three times in a row!

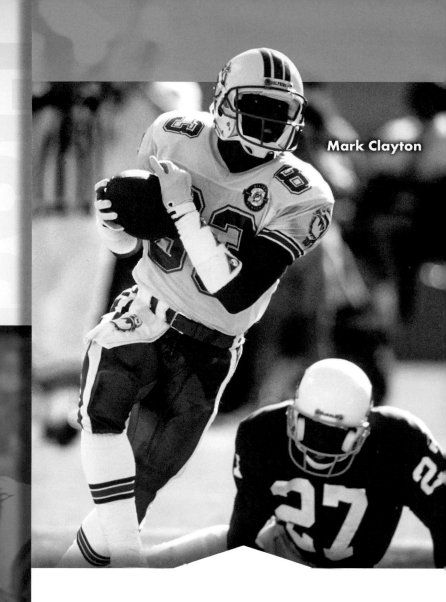

Mark Clayton

Dan Marino led the team
in the 1980s and 1990s.
He often looked for **wide
receiver** Mark Clayton.
These two helped the team
rise to the top of the AFC.

Over the years, the Dolphins have had strong **defenses**. Fans cheered the "No-Name Defense" in the 1970s. In the early 1980s, the "Killer B's" were hard to face.

In 2003, **defensive end** Jason Taylor beat the team's all-time **sack** record. He also set an NFL record with his sixth **fumble** return for a touchdown in 2009.

TEAM GREATS

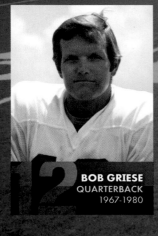

BOB GRIESE
QUARTERBACK
1967-1980

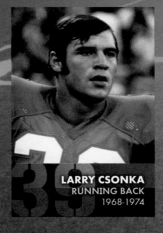

LARRY CSONKA
RUNNING BACK
1968-1974

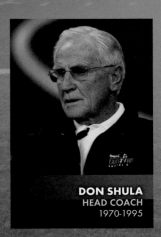

DON SHULA
HEAD COACH
1970-1995

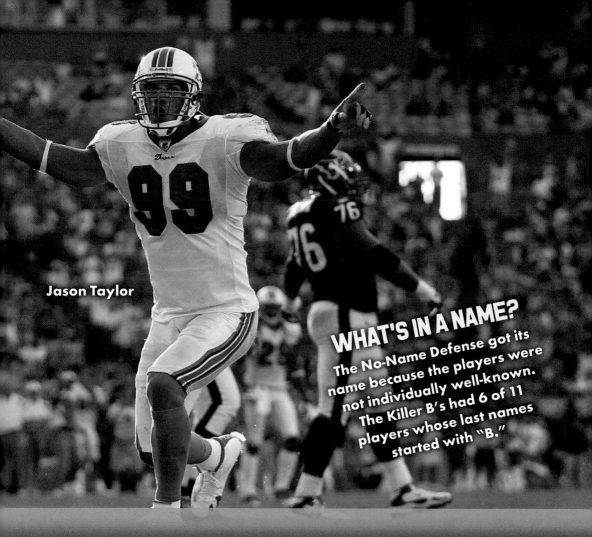

Jason Taylor

WHAT'S IN A NAME?

The No-Name Defense got its name because the players were not individually well-known. The Killer B's had 6 of 11 players whose last names started with "B."

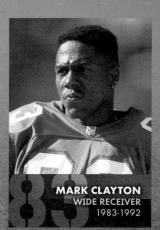

MARK CLAYTON
WIDE RECEIVER
1983-1992

DAN MARINO
QUARTERBACK
1983-1999

JASON TAYLOR
DEFENSIVE END
1997-2007, 2009, 2011

The Dolphins' bright colors represent the team's home state. Aqua is like the color of the ocean. Orange matches the sun.

Their logo shows a dolphin just before it leaps out of the water. This is a dolphin's most powerful moment.

FLIPPING FOR THE TEAM

From 1966 to 1968, the Dolphins' stadium had a live dolphin named Flipper. The dolphin did tricks when the team scored.

After the 1990s, the Dolphins have had tough seasons. But the team mascot, T.D., helps fans cheer on their team.

T.D.

True fans stick it out during hard times. They will be the ones celebrating most when the next **dynasty** comes.

MORE ABOUT THE
DOLPHINS

Team name:
Miami Dolphins

Team name explained:
**Named after the fast
bottlenose dolphin**

**Nicknames: Killer B's, The
Fins, No-Name Defense**

**Joined NFL: 1970
(AFL from 1966-1969)**

Conference: AFC

Division: East

Main rivals:
Buffalo Bills, New York Jets

Hometown:
Miami Gardens, Florida

Training camp location: Doctors Hospital Training Facility, Nova Southeastern University, Davie, Florida

FLORIDA

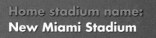

N
W — E
S

MIAMI GARDENS

Home stadium name:
New Miami Stadium

Stadium opened: 1987

Seats in stadium: 65,326

Logo: An aqua dolphin in front of a sunburst

Colors: Aqua, marine blue, orange, white

Mascot: T.D.

GLOSSARY

canopy—a hanging shelter or cover

conference—a large grouping of sports teams that often play one another

defenses—groups of players who try to stop the opposing team from scoring

defensive end—a player on defense whose job is to tackle the player with the ball

division—a small grouping of sports teams that often play one another; usually there are several divisions of teams in a conference.

dynasty—a team that succeeds for many years

expansion team—a new team added to a sports league

fumble—a loose ball that is still in play

legendary—famous for being good at something

offense—the group of players who try to move down the field and score

playoffs—the games played after the regular NFL season is over; playoff games determine which teams play in the Super Bowl.

quarterback—a player on offense whose main job is to throw and hand off the ball

rival—a long-standing opponent

sack—a play during which a player on defense tackles the opposing quarterback for a loss of yards

Super Bowl—the championship game for the NFL

tight end—a player on offense whose main jobs are to catch the ball and block for teammates

wide receiver—a player on offense whose main job is to catch passes from the quarterback

winning record—when a team has more wins than losses in a season

TO LEARN MORE

AT THE LIBRARY

Whiting, Jim. *The Story of the Miami Dolphins*. Mankato, Minn.: Creative Education, 2014.

Wyner, Zach. *Miami Dolphins*. New York, N.Y.: AV2 by Weigl, 2015.

Zappa, Marcia. *Miami Dolphins*. Edina, Minn.: ABDO Pub. Company, 2015.

ON THE WEB

Learning more about the Miami Dolphins is as easy as 1, 2, 3.

1. Go to www.factsurfer.com.

2. Enter "Miami Dolphins" into the search box.

3. Click the "Surf" button and you will see a list of related web sites.

With factsurfer.com, finding more information is just a click away.

INDEX